BÔ YIN RÂ
(J. A. SCHNEIDERFRANKEN)

THE GATED GARDEN
VOLUME SIX

THE PATH TO GOD

For more information
about the books of Bô Yin Râ and
titles published in English translation,
visit The Kober Press web site at
www.kober.com.

BÔ YIN RÂ
(J. A. SCHNEIDERFRANKEN)

THE PATH TO GOD

TRANSLATED FROM THE GERMAN
BY B.A. REICHENBACH

THE
KOBER
PRESS

BERKELEY, CALIFORNIA

For permission to quote or excerpt, write to:

THE KOBER PRESS
2534 Chilton Way
Berkeley, California 94704

email: koberpress@mindspring.com

This book is a translation from the German of *Der Weg zu Gott* by Bô Yin Râ (J.A. Schneiderfranken), published in 1924 by Rhein-Verlag A.-G. Basle. The copyright to the German text is held by Kober Verlag, AG, Bern, Switzerland.

Printed in the United States of America

International Standard Book Number: 978-0-915034-15-8

Typography and composition by Dickie Magidoff, Burney, CA

Book cover after a design by Bô Yin Râ

ACKNOWLEDGMENT

For her careful reading
and many perceptive comments
I continue to be grateful to
Alice Glawe

CONTENTS

"I FIND YOU ALWAYS IN A RUSH, MY FRIEND! TELL ME, WHAT IS THE GOAL YOU SEEK TO REACH IN SUCH A HURRY?"

Many times I asked this question, and I was given many different answers.

Sadly, very few appeared to recognize that all the goals they strove to reach were merely substitutes, since they had lost the way that leads to the eternal goal they once had meant to reach:

THE PATH TO GOD

CHAPTER ONE

FANTASY AND FAITH

H ERE I DO NOT MEAN TO RAISE the question whether there is "need" for mortal human beings to believe in "God."

All who made their living by promoting this belief have always, and in every corner of the globe, insisted that the answer must be: Yes! Such unanimity, however, has long since cast widespread suspicion not only on the question itself, but equally on every answer.

What I shall ask instead is how, and under what conditions, it is possible for any human mortal even to proclaim that he "believes" in GOD.

THERE ARE AMONG the "sacred" books of ancient peoples not a few where you can read that long ago, in one place or another, a "God" had personally appeared to a believer.

If a mortal having had such luck then claims that he believes in this particular "God" he well may be entitled, in his own mind, to hold to this belief.

Whatever had in fact "appeared" to him, he took the apparition to be "God." If now he claims that he "believes," he says no more than that he saw an apparition and does not recognize the self-delusion which causes him to think that what he saw was "God."

But how can you, a person who has never had the like experience, come to claim that you believe in God?

You merely shaped yourself a "God" in your own likeness—out of thoughts.

You raised your own self to perfection in an image, and this mentally constructed concept you revere as "God."

What you worship is an idol you created; and so you made yourself the servant of your own imagination.

Unable to escape your own inherent limitations, you made yourself your narrow comprehension's thrall.

In the same way as you must yourself create whatever you would see created, you speculate there also must be One who, like yourself, brought forth this great wide world, which you experience through your senses; and this assumed creator, who merely is the work of your constricted vision, you look upon as "God"; the commitment to your own delusion is what you call your "faith."

Within the world that here surrounds you from without you see that many things appear designed as if they were to serve a given purpose; and since you, too, as a component of this selfsame world, are seeking to achieve your aims by suitable means, you now surmise there also must be One behind the things you see who, like yourself, has aims he is determined to achieve.

It does not trouble you that obviously the greater part of this external world appears in conflict with such ultimate design, and that the purposeful "creator" would have to be a quite pathetic bungler, far more inept than even his supposed "creature," if he could be inferred, as your delusion would persuade you, from a work that reaches certain goals but manifestly fails in others.

Nor does it trouble you that much too often that which you perceived as *purpose* is accomplished only to the end of being once again destroyed by something else, which you observe to be no less intended for some *purpose*.

This gives you pause. But never at a loss for explanations, you let your fantasy suppose a "wisdom of inscrutable profundity," but which cannot make sense without the aid of nonsense.

You have observed that mortal man through all of history and in all peoples of the earth envisioned some superior force in order to obey and worship what he had envisioned; and, consequently, you conclude that your imagined deity must somehow correspond to a reality. And given that your mind was able to create him out of thoughts you now "believe" the "God" whom you created actually *exists*, and many things you learned to say about his nature.

Modest you are truly not; and for all your glorified "humility before the Lord," you do not realize how curiously you base your "God's" existence on your own.

You recognize that you live here on earth; and so the "God" of your creation *must*—because you so decree—exist somewhere in "heaven."

Whether you merely repeat what others have told you about "God," his attributes, and nature, or whether you dismiss such ancient pious lore, preferring to allow your own thoughts to envision "God"—in either case you are the captive of the same hypnotic circle, which your overweening superstition made you draw; even if you deem yourself above the bonds of all "beliefs" and feel your mind and thoughts are "free."

OF SUCH DELUSIONS I would have you cured, my friend; and I will show you that despite all false ideas it nonetheless is possible for mortals to "believe in God."

I mean to show you that the One you should believe in is a "God" who is not simply the invention of your own or someone else's colorful imagination; a "God," instead, whose absolute reality no depth of mental logic ever fathoms nor can "prove."

First of all, however, we here need to agree between us on what the concept "God" is meant to signify.

That I do not employ the word denoting "God" to mean a phantom of misguided thought, a specter seeming real only to deluded minds, you have been shown already by the lucid background of my opening remarks.

The reality that we want to approach transcends all mental comprehension.

The One whose Being is eternal we want to meet on our path. If you would recognize and know him, your inner eye needs to be clear and free of fanciful mirages.

The images of thought your mind produced, you must from now on set aside.

What you shall encounter is the Oneness that beside its own self knows no other, but which reveals its unity in infinitely varied individuations wherever it can manifest its essence to itself.

You are yourself its living revelation, although you are not conscious of it yet; and in yourself alone can the reality that would reveal itself in fact be comprehended—within the conscious life that is revealed.

It was within yourself that you had faced illusion; now, however, you likewise shall within yourself encounter truth.

You will not find it very difficult to tell the truth from what is merely self-deception.

Those who had deceived themselves, but then awakened from their dreams, often lost all courage; and now they fear they might fall prey to new deceptions. Thus, truth itself, if ever it were to confront them, will face an uphill battle, lest it be dismissed as simply a mirage.

You must not follow their example and let bitterness deter you; for though you may have failed in your endeavor nine-and-ninety times, success may still be yours the hundredth time you try.

Who can be certain that before today you would have recognized the truth, if your time to meet it had not come?

Perhaps in your impatience to encounter truth you sought it on a path it must avoid?

Finding yourself on the right path, however, and being prepared to face it, you truly shall no longer be in doubt whether that which manifests itself within you is eternal truth indeed or merely a mirage of your own mind.

In that which in yourself is *of the truth* will timeless truth reveal its presence.

The light that is the source of all illumination shall henceforth shine within you; and all the lamps you once had lit to help you find your way, you then will scarcely notice, guided by the radiance in yourself.

You shall encounter your own life in its eternal, infinite abundance. Rising from the dead by light's awakening power you will behold your resurrection from the darkness of your earthly grave.

With "God," the Ground of Being sustaining all existence, you shall find yourself in unity.

Addressing your own self as "*I*," you will gain understanding that His name is to be "hallowed."

Even as you hear me speaking to you in this way, you feel the stirrings of a living force within you; be it that you sense it strongly, or that at first it knocks but timidly upon your heart's securely bolted portal.

There is within you something that more clearly hears my words than does your earthly mind, which merely seeks to analyze their meaning.

That very "something" is the energy of *faith*, which dwells in you, but to your consciousness is still unknown.

Perhaps you scarcely can believe that you can find it in yourself.

From childhood on you have excessively relied upon the faculty of thinking and thus became convinced that final certainty in every field, to the extent at least that mortals may approach it, can only be attained by thought.

Now many times your thinking has betrayed you; and to this day you are in bondage to your thought.

Yet even so you fear that you might plunge into a groundless void if you were ever to have trust in anything except your thinking mind.

It is nothing but that fear which will not let you put your trust in faith's dynamic energy.

However, you shall hear me speak to you in vain as long as you will only use your mind to grasp my words and seek to prove them merely by your thoughts.

Do NOT ASSUME that here I mean to denigrate the faculty of thought!

I know full well that there is much in mortal life which only trained and skillful thinking can unlock; and deeply I respect what mankind owes to its outstanding thinkers.

But one thing is what thought can generate and grasp and quite another that which faith's capacity alone can make you apprehend.

You surely recognize that here I do not speak about the kind of "faith" that but *assumes* whatever it "believes."

Such tentative assuming is unworthy, in my judgment, to bear the name of "faith."

The energy of faith that I speak of instead is wholly different in nature.

There is no place in it for speculating and assuming, nor for opinions and deductions. Those who will entrust themselves to the dynamic energy of faith, even if at first they sense it only in its faintest form, shall truly not be bound to hold some creed.

They soon will grow aware, however, that within them is at work a power that may lead them to discover more than one new insight, which "flesh and blood" would never have revealed.

What now you may feel stirring in yourself, although you are not able to explain it, is the very energy of faith, perhaps still in its weakest form.

There is within you something that would like to give consent to what I said above, if but your thoughts were not attempting to hold you back by all kinds of objections.

If you are satisfied forever to remain in bondage to your thoughts you will have little to expect from the dynamic energy of faith, which wants to see you free of any chains.

Only if you can unchain yourself from bondage to your thoughts will you experience faith's dynamic energy at work within your being.

You would surely laugh at any craftsman who took an axe to split a beam of steel and madness would you see displayed if someone used a saw to cut through panes of glass.

But until now you have attempted something very similar; and still you do not realize how thoroughly you led yourself astray.

With means that are intrinsically unfitting you struggle to achieve what cannot ever be achieved that way.

You are attempting, as it were, to fell an oak tree with a pocket knife and with bare hands you try to dig for ore.

I am obliged to tell you, however, that the faculty of reasoning, although a tried and tested tool when probing things of earthly life, is bound to prove inadequate the moment you decide to strive for knowledge that is rooted in the Spirit.

Here, the energy of faith alone is able to provide you help.

Do not suppose it might prove less effective in guiding you to certainty than rational thinking will—in the domain where it alone presents the fitting tool.

You still connect the meaning of the word "believe" with only the idea of "thinking to be true" of that which is "believed," or thought to be "believed." The energy of faith, however, imparts an inner certainty that one is *able to attain* the goal that faith has promised.

If thus you shall "believe" in God you surely will no longer trust the claims of those who have no more to offer you as "truth" than phantoms hatched within the narrow confines of their comprehension.

You will believe but your own self when trusting the dynamic energy of faith.

Within you shall you recognize that energy at work; and what it would reveal to you has in your own self its foundation.

Within yourself shall you *experience* the teachings of that energy.

Only what you shall *experience* in yourself, my friend, will truly be your own.

Things of which you cannot be as sure as you are of your earthly body you ought not to regard as "certain."

What you cannot apprehend as clearly as you grasp yourself you have not truly apprehended.

You should not say that you "believe" what you cannot "believe" as certainly as you "believe" that you exist.

I WANT TO GUIDE you toward authentic "faith" —a faith for which you can accept responsibility before your heart and mind.

I want to guide you to a faith that you shall never question nor renounce.

The faith to which I want to guide you shall outlive your mortal days on earth.

Only then will you indeed be able to declare that truth *compels* you to believe in "God."

And not before shall also He, in whose existence you "believe," acknowledge you as a "believer."

Before that day, however, all "professions of faith" are merely empty phrases; are nothing more than your assenting to your own or someone else's fantasies, imagined to be holy.

But having once experienced what can in truth be known, you henceforth shall be free of all delusions.

Once you have discovered what the energy of faith alone is able to unfold to your experience you will have gained a certainty that one can never take from you again in all eternity.

Having entrusted yourself to the power of faith, you truly shall one day attain the certainty that justifies your making the profession:

"I believe in God!"

&

CHAPTER TWO

KNOWING CERTAINTY

YOU TRULY NEVER SHALL REACH final certainty of knowledge unless the energy of faith will first illuminate your path.

Let me tell you that I myself had once pursued erroneous paths when I had not yet known the self I am.

I, too, had been my own delusions' slave until the time that I was found by those who had already counted me among their kind long before I first experienced life in a material body and as a mortal human being.

I truly may bear witness of that which leads to certainty, given that I earlier was forced to recognize the power of delusion.

Those who follow my advice shall be securely guided.

I truly came to know the way that leads to final certainty, for I myself had to become the "way" before the task was given me to show that path to others.

I had awakened and grown conscious of myself within the radiance of eternal light and only then did it become my obligation also to bring light to those who still abide in darkness.

Then only was it made my duty to awaken all those whom my words may reach and wrest them from their dreams in darkness.

BEFORE I COULD reach certainty of knowledge, I, too, once had to put my trust in faith's dynamic power.

And greater trust was demanded of me than you will ever be expected to display.

There was a day when I had to prepare myself to leave this earthly life forever; and nothing but the energy of faith was able then to motivate me to endure a trial whose outcome could have ended my existence here on earth, even as in truth it granted me—not envisioned at the time and certainly not known —fully conscious and awakened life.

I thus may certainly assure you that one can put one's trust in faith's dynamic power.

And further I may tell you that you will fathom certainty of knowledge in proportion to your confidence in the dynamic energy of faith.

"Faith" and "knowledge," here, do not by any means exist in opposition, because what I call "faith" is the enabling requisite for your attaining "knowledge."

The energy of faith alone creates the possibility within you that certainty of knowledge can in fact be yours.

As long as you still harbor doubts and will not put your trust in faith's dynamic energy you have no rightful claim to be among the ones who "know."

One may compare this mutual dependence to a chain whose links are intertwined.

Trust in the dynamic energy of faith is necessary; and that same energy of faith creates in you the confidence you need if you would come to certainty of knowledge.

"Knowledge," here, is not the recognition of phenomena that may be causally connected.

"Knowledge," here, is the *experience* of an inner certainty that is completely free of doubt, securely anchored in itself.

Whoever reaches knowledge of that nature will treat the "proof" required by the mortal mind's pursuit of knowledge as no more than a temporary substitute, which he can do without because the knowledge he possesses is at the same time proof of what he knows.

Even as a person pressing the buzzer of a doorbell does not require "proof" that now a signal might be heard; and as that person likewise need not have the slightest understanding of the specific laws that bring about the ringing of the bell, so will a human being capable of *knowing* in the Spirit be conscious of his knowledge without "proof" and unconcerned about the causal links that are required to make him conscious of his knowledge.

WHOEVER WOULD GAIN certainty of knowledge much in the way a person having eyes can see, although he might be quite unable to explain how vision is created, that person has no choice but to accept the fact that he will not receive his knowledge without assistance from a higher source; even as a mortal having eyesight will have to be content that his ability to see depends on the performance of a delicate and easily injured organ of his body.

In either case there are conditions that must have been fulfilled if the desired purpose is to be achieved.

The smallest clouding of your eye will either rob you of your vision or seriously obstruct it. Thanks only to the function of a small organ of your physical body do you possess the gift of sight.

And if you, in addition, would observe a distant star or recognize minutest particles of matter, you even need the help of optical instruments, which human ingenuity invented and learned to manufacture.

All that appears to you entirely in order; and surely you would not expect that even without eyes you should be capable of seeing; nor that the rings of Saturn would reveal themselves to you without assistance from a telescope.

Indeed, you long ago have recognized that even the most powerful of telescopes will never show you the remotest stars, and also that the very sharpest microscope will not suffice to let you see the tiniest of particles, whose presence you are able to infer, although no human eye has ever seen them.

Within the Spirit's life, however, you assume you have no need of any help.

You treat your "God" as merely good enough to be addressed with the familiar "thou" and —having lost all sense of distance and proportion in your hubris—presumptuously demand that nothing else should stand between yourself and him.

You resemble the infant reaching for the moon, because it seems no further from its grasp than does the toy suspended for its pleasure in the window.

On earth you readily acknowledge immense distinctions in significance and rank among your fellow mortals.

However you may call the "great" and "powerful" before whose might you bow—all of them are merely mortals like yourself; even though you feel they rank ahead of you in knowledge and ability, in wisdom and potential, or merely in hereditary privilege.

How very low must your opinion be of the dimension of the Spirit if you do not even vaguely sense that also in that realm one rank succeeds another; and that an almost endless hierarchy ascends before the highest princes in the Spirit can be reached who, living in the Godhead's inmost light, in truth reflect the image human intuition fathomed of the "cherubim" and "seraphim."

"Princes" have evolved among your kind; and if you rank creative genius of the human spirit higher than all dignity of princes you know of mortals who accomplished all but superhuman works in fields that you on earth consider "spiritual"; but even the greatest whom you thus may venerate had barely reached, when he was still alive on earth, the very lowest rank of those who are alive already in the Spirit's radiant substance.

How then can you presume that you, a mortal who will even here on earth give way and bow to higher power are so close already to your "God" that nothing else could find its place between yourself and him?

To be sure, if "God" is no more than the idol you created in your image, then your demand is justified.

Yet if you seek to unify yourself with your eternal living GOD, who without end abides in Being through the aeons, and will reveal himself within you, then you must forget this foolish notion.

Out of your own self you then shall learn to apprehend that here you are in need of help; once having recognized that need, however, you will receive the help that you require.

To everyone desiring help it shall indeed be given.

The primordial Light of the Beginning, which you presume so readily accessible to your perception, without all intermediaries, itself brought forth such helpers on this planet; and they know how to reach you as soon as you are willing to be reached.

About this help I told you much in other books in different words and images; here I will consider more the inner state you need to make your own if you resolve to enter and pursue your path to God.

Once you have entered the path you soon will grow aware that you can go no further without assistance from a higher source.

As soon as you have recognized that truth you will be ready to receive it.

Do not concern yourself about the way in which this help from higher realms is being sent to you.

Feel assured, however, through the energy of faith within yourself, that such help must reach you.

You then are certain to receive it, even though you never could suspect the source from where it reaches you.

Only with this inner help shall you attain the certainty of knowledge.

YOU WELL MAY think, if you believe your first impression, that what you apprehend are insights merely of your own perception; and so you are unlikely to suspect that someone else is speaking to you in your soul; one of those who live on earth but at the same time are awake and conscious in the world of Spirit, albeit only on the lowest rung of the eternal hierarchy, whose higher ranks you could not reach except through them while you still live on earth in mortal form.

Such help you will experience only in your highest moments, whether you are able to discern its source or not.

But then you once more shall endure the times of gloom and darkness and you will groan in your distress.

You then will feel as if "by God forsaken," not knowing where to look for shelter and support.

Still, at such times you never must lose courage!

You then will unexpectedly once more experience the guidance of that inner "voice" and all the anguish that had burdened you will slowly leave you and dissolve.

Determination leads you to your goal and you will grow aware that higher powers are guiding your ascent.

YOU ARE PREPARED by virtue of the energy inherent in dynamic faith.

You now desire to gain certainty of knowledge.

You shall in truth attain it if you but seek it in yourself.

As long as you still hesitate and stumble, not knowing what indeed you want, you shall in vain seek to discover certainty of knowledge.

You first need to grow certain of yourself if you desire to be raised to certainty of spiritual knowledge in the Spirit's realm.

But having put your trust in the dynamic energy of faith, you truly shall have grown in being certain of yourself.

Within your inmost self shall you discover the fountain of all wisdom. The *knowledge* that you shall attain within yourself you never could acquire in the world without.

Within yourself alone, my friend, can you *experience* certainty.

❧

CHAPTER THREE

DREAMING SOULS

CONFINED WITHIN THE EARTHLY CREATURE'S physical perception, the souls inhabiting this earth are dreaming in the depth of sleep which they impose upon themselves by their own will.

All their physical "experience" is no more than a dream until they shall awaken.

Asleep they cannot comprehend what fully conscious and awake experience truly is.

Only one who has awakened is able to distinguish between experience of reality and the deceptive world of self-created phantoms appearing in his dreams.

Very seldom does the consciousness that he is dreaming surface in the dreamer's sleep.

But firmly in the dream world's grip the energy is lacking to escape its hold.

Too deep in many cases is the dreamers' sleep, too thoroughly will it protect the sleepers' dreams even when reality's explicit wake-up call is heard by them while sleeping.

To awaken sleeping souls appears almost impossible. Each such awakening is not unlike a "miracle."

For dreaming is the state that souls desire.

They lack the will to end their sleep and to awaken.

Enraptured by the world of dreams, sleeping souls are fearful, dreading the end of their dreams.

Only things they can experience in their dreams they deem "experience" that is worth their while.

They shudder at the thought of having to abandon their dreams.

Each dreaming soul creates its own distinctive world, even though the same world may be formed in dreams by many.

And in the same way will each soul create its own inscrutable and distant "God," residing in a world above, infinities beyond all reach, without suspecting that it merely shaped a heightened likeness of itself and in that image thus reveres and worships its own self.

How should the soul be able to discern that first it would have to awaken before it could within itself encounter its Living God "to worship him in spirit and in truth?"

In bondage to the outer world of dreams it seeks without itself what it can only find *within*; indeed, exclusively within the *inmost* of its inner self.

It mentally projects its inner self into the outer world; and infinitely farther still, beyond the stars, creates the image of a "God" in its own likeness; a "God" who merely is the product of mortal human folly.

THAT DREAM WORKS a beguiling spell on human souls and keeps them sleeping longer than there would be need.

Too seductive are the dream world's colorful mirages, and so they even keep those souls asleep who otherwise might well awaken, because in them already has begun to stir the will to wake up from their sleep.

Not before the sleeper's own will to awaken makes him rise can he escape from dreams he has himself created.

If, like a sleeper startled by a strident waking call, he drowsily would wrest himself from sleep before his time, he soon would only fall asleep again, a captive of his dreams.

Even in its dream-life, to be sure, the soul's desire is to know the world of truth and of reality.

Yet easily it can delude itself and thus believe its own self is awake and that, instead, reality is but a dream

And without question it is easier to dream that one is close to, indeed united with a phantom "God" of one's imagination, than it is to follow, free of all illusions, the path that none is able to pursue except *within*, and which at last will lead, within the inmost of one's inner self, to the desired goal: eternal union with the Living God.

THE RAPTURES OF their dreams unduly have elated also those who tell about their having in themselves encountered "God" and thus have now become themselves completely "god-like" in their being.

Excitedly they dream beguiling dreams and in their sleep believe they have awakened, unsuspecting that their "god-like" state is but a phantom of their dream.

Yet truth, my friend, is very different. When you shall know the Living God within yourself—as your *own* inherent Living God—you shall indeed experience him in only your own self, and your own self at one with him, but you will not have thus become a "God," nor "god-like" in your nature.

You then shall certainly at all times be "in God" and live in God's eternal life, but you shall not yourself be "God" nor ever will be in eternity.

What you are able to experience is yourself in God and your eternal Living God within yourself—in consciousness of unified experience—and yet you always shall remain the one you are.

God, however, comes to know himself in you as in an "image," such as Godhead never could experience its own Being in itself; even as the sunlight's rays, when gathered in a lens, will in its focal point transform their light to fire.

It is your mind, my friend, that prompts you to conclude that "if there is a God," then you as well, once unified with him, ought to be able one day to become a "God."

Your thoughts, however, are in bondage to your dreams, given that they are your dreams' creations.

Do not assume that you are close to your awakening as long as you regard your thinking as your brightest source of light. In the world of matter, where your thinking is at home, it doubtless may prove of great service and I surely would not denigrate its worth. In the darkness of a coal mine's tunnel in the bowels of the earth I definitely shall value a lamp that miners use. But even as a miner's torch would quickly pale if, having risen to the surface in the light of day, one were to use it in the blinding brilliance of the summer sun, even so all thinking loses its effectiveness when it presumes to shed its light upon the clarity in which awakened spiritual perception apprehends reality.

You ought to use and profit from your thinking wherever it may serve your aims—but you should not remain the dream-enraptured captive of your thoughts!

In the darkness, deep within the labyrinthian tunnels of physical experience, you surely will at all times need the lantern of your thinking mind; but once ascended to the light of day within the Spirit's sun you confidently may extinguish the smoldering flame that only shines in darkness; for here you are surrounded by the radiance of another light, one you do not need to kindle, nor protect.

Awakening within that light you then will recognize the folly of your wanting to illuminate the very rays of the sun with an oil lamp's feeble glimmer.

THE DREAMS BEGUILING souls are manifold in content; nor are they all removed alike from consciously experiencing reality.

Much as in your body's sleep each night some echoes of the outer world may drift into your dreams and then, in dream-like transformation, can impress your consciousness, so is there likewise many an echo of awakened spiritual perception sounding in the dreams of souls.

Such a dream may then become a distant premonition of awakened life, but even so it merely stays a dream.

Perhaps you have yourself already come to know such echoes in the dream-life of your soul?

Perhaps you even felt that now you were yourself not far from your awakening, only to succumb once more to dreaming in your sleep?

At least you may consider that a sign that you are close to your awakening, although perhaps not quite so close as you would like to think.

Make it more and more your practice, even in your dream and in your dream-life's self-sufficiency, to listen for the echoes from the Spirit's world, where all life is awake.

Even if at first you cannot hear them other than transposed according to your dream-life's key, they nonetheless shall cause you to awaken more and more, until at last they guide you to the bliss of your complete awakening.

Step by step you are to be awakened from your dream.

Your awakening must not be brought about by sudden shock.

One does not want to find you in confusion when you awaken from your many-colored life-long dream.

For even your awakening could then prove harmful to your soul.

The all-exceeding brightness of the Spirit's light at first must be endured before one grows to love it.

Only then shall you be able to endure it if gradually awakening you broke the fetters of your sleep.

IF ON THE OTHER hand you are today still fast asleep and live a dream no echo from the

Spirit's fully wakened world can pierce, or, if you heard its sound, you judged it a disturbing interruption of your sleep, then let this tell you that "your time" is still far off; for you could not yet be awakened from your sleep without sustaining shock.

Even if one could awaken you, you would not stay awake for more than fleeting moments and very soon would once again surrender to the lure of sleep.

I only would advise you gradually to get accustomed to the sounds you now still feel to be "disruption."

Do not become too much enamored of your dream, but ask yourself if you could not envision that for you as well the time must come when you shall finally awaken.

Thus you will in time regard the echoes from the Spirit's fully wakened world as less and less disruptive; your dream will grow increasingly more lucid, and finally you shall come ever closer to your own awakening.

IT IS NOT A PLAY with empty words when I compare the life of those who are not yet awake and fully conscious in the Spirit to the state of sleep, and call the mental world of their conceptions an elusive dream.

As I address myself to humans here on earth I must employ analogies that mortal humans understand.

Anyone, however, who may in the future read these words will also have experienced sleep and dreams.

But even as you would consider any person foolish who claimed that only in his sleep he truly is awake and that his dreams alone presented the reality of earthly life, so should you likewise learn to recognize that this material life of physical perception does not by any means comprise the highest level of reality; and also that what here you call "experience" and "perception" lags far behind the way in which you will experience and perceive in the dynamic substance of the Spirit's world if once you have yourself awakened in the Spirit's realm, even though you still continue living as a mortal human in the world that earthly senses apprehend.

Blest you will be knowing you pursue the path that in yourself shall let you apprehend the Spirit's world as one who has awakened.

Blest you will be even if at least you recognize that such a path has been prepared for your ascent as well.

Although today you still may feel that you are far from the beginning of that path, the very knowledge that this path exists will lend you strength to enter it, defying every obstacle; and if you know that you have entered it already, you also know that all you need to do is resolutely to pursue it and thus shall come to God within yourself.

∞

CHAPTER FOUR

TRUTH AND REALITY

W HATEVER CONCEPT IN THE REALM of your ideas you find so deeply rooted that no endeavor of your thinking ever could dislodge it from its base you look upon as "true." You also recognize as "truth," however, any number of conceptual constructs which you today and with your present mental powers were unable to depose. Yet if such concepts are later overthrown by other minds, their "truth" has ceased to be reality for you as well.

And so we see how each succeeding generation protected its own truth like an immortal treasure, seeking carefully to guard it for the age to follow, while the latter would regard that heritage as having no more usefulness than children's toys.

Yet even so, "the truth" as such has to this day remained a highly prized commodity, although at times it seemed unclear which concept at a given moment was to be considered "truth."

IF HERE WE ARE to speak of *truth* we purposely shall leave aside whatever in the course of time may have been held to be the "truth."

Here we shall accept as truth no more than that which every age, besides its own time's closely bound opinions, had known as truth that could not be disproved by later generations.

Applying this criterion, one may regard the fact as truth that mortal human knowledge gained by thinking remains forever incomplete; and likewise, that man's power over nature, despite all triumphs in exploiting natural forces, must all too soon acknowledge limitations, which human will had not imposed upon itself.

This truth led human thinking to conclude that those domains of knowledge and of power which mortals are unable to attain are under the control of someone else's will and might.

But with this notion one creates a mental image that is easily dethroned again because it lacks the fundament that might support the "truth" suggesting this conclusion.

While thought and logical deductions are able to design conceptual analogies one may regard as truth's most fitting likeness, the truth itself, as here it should be understood, will never be unlocked by thinking or by logic.

FINAL TRUTH RESTS far beyond and high above all thinking; nor can it ever be approached by thought—unless a person came to *face* reality within, and thus objectively *experienced* what was sought, so that he then may grant it to his thinking as a gift.

Innumerable times have mortal minds constructed "God" through thinking and believed they had encountered "God" by means of thought.

Yet even thinking of the subtlest kind created but an idol in the human mortal's image; a mental construct thriving merely in the phantom world of human thought, a sense-inspired, sense-devoid mirage.

Little wonder that in every age there have been those who would refuse to put their faith in such a "God." On the other hand, it all but passes comprehension that such a mentally conceived mirage was able, time and time again, to find believers who in devotion bowed their heads before its power.

VERY FEW WERE those in any age who in this matter wanted neither to believe nor to deny, but simply turned their backs on the imagined phantom of the mind, so that they might within themselves *experience* their living God in his sublime reality.

What is experienced in this way will necessarily reduce all mental concepts to mere mockery.

No concept can be formed that might reflect the truth of this experience. No thought is able to present its likeness, nor can it be conveyed through words.

None but those embracing this experience *know* about its nature; and thus they also know—by virtue solely of that personal experience—that they in truth encounter what not merely bears the name of "God," but that which Godhead is within itself through all eternity.

Gnawing doubt, which threatens even the profoundest insight of a lucid mind, has here no longer any force, because one thus awakens to the inmost Ground of Being within one's own eternal self.

Even as a light that has been lit inside a lamp will show the color of the panes through which it passes, yet is itself not colored by the nature of the lamp, so will the Godhead enter the human being's inmost self, will manifest itself therein according to that being's individuality, and yet remain what it forever was and is.

United with its timeless Ground of Being in such absolute reality, the human being's individuated consciousness at last will recognize the real nature of eternal truth and, equally, that truth's innate reality.

Here only will the human self grow conscious of *God's* essence in *truth* and in *reality*. All mental images of God believed in earlier days have now dissolved in darkening twilight. Whoever thus *experiences* the Godhead in himself, and his own self's reality within it, clearly has no longer need of similes and parables; only when instructing others must he choose descriptive language, so that his words may activate their intuition.

Still, all the images he may employ remain a stammering attempt at explanation; even if he sought to give account of this experience employing every kind of imagery that language has to offer.

ONLY THOSE WHO thus have in reality *experienced* their own *living God* within themselves can truly know of God with certainty; and they alone, indeed, know also of themselves with final certainty.

Yet even this superior level of attainment is merely preparation for every subsequent unfolding in the Spirit's world. Still, very few in any age have ever reached it in their mortal lives, let alone surpassed it.

It is a crime to speak of God, and if it were in words of matchless eloquence, unless the speaker knows, with certainty beyond all doubt, that he has truly reached this level.

But having truly reached it, he shall also have discovered whether he in fact is called upon to teach; and only those who can speak with authority shall not profane the name of God.

To him it "shall be given" what he is to say —by those who have been granted more than he, in that they had already, millennia ago, been found upon the path that he has only learned about today.

One cannot possibly experience one's own living God within and not be conscious of the guidance offered by those who work as mankind's *elder brothers* in the Spirit.

They, too, had once depended on such guidance when they pursued their path, until they reached the union with their living God within themselves.

Much more had been demanded of them, however, given that they were to work as helpers of all human souls surrounded by the threat of night.

Burdens of far greater weight were they compelled to bear.

Thus were they made capable, already in their days on earth, of entering the Spirit's world awake and fully conscious; the very world of radiant spiritual substance they had known, and which had been their home, long before they would receive their earthly bodies in this present world as mortal human beings.

What many an ancient legend, which until now you may have mocked as "foolish," has nonetheless to tell you, if in shrouded language, is left to your own searching, given that you now have learned of their existence.

As for myself, however, I here can only tell you that I speak from *final certainty*, as one whose words convey objective personal experience.

If ever in this mortal life you truly want to know your *living God* you must not spurn the help provided by your *elder brothers*, who already live within the Spirit's world. Their help is shunned by those, however, who in their search for God explore all heights and depths, but cannot break the bondage of their mental pride, whose constant flattery persuades them to believe they have no need of any help that human beings offer from the Spirit.

Seeking to encounter *spiritual reality* within yourself, you must not turn away from what that same *reality* has brought into existence.

Not you are going to decide how God is to awaken in your consciousness—but God!

It is not "human help" that reaches you when you receive the Spirit's help through human beings, to which I here refer, but help of *God*, which thus avails itself of human beings in order to reach mortal humans, who in their creature life on earth would not in any other way be able to receive God's help.

One does not here expect you simply to "believe," as if you had to trust my words for their own sake; I merely tell you what necessity demands, without exception, if you in truth intend to *find*, not only *seek*!

Nothing more is asked of you than that you will not stubbornly refuse the help, which — purely in the Spirit's way—can *spiritually* reach you. Whether my words deserve "belief," let those confirm who put them into practice—then go and prove them by your own experience!

I do not mean to offer you some new "belief," but seek instead to guide your soul to *certainty*: to that objective *truth* which is experienced only as *reality*.

You will be able to gather and to unify your soul's dynamic energies within you only if the rivers flowing from the Spirit's life will nourish you with strength; yet these inner currents are conveyed into the night of physical existence by those who work as *mediators* from the Spirit's world, because this is their given task and duty.

They are themselves but instruments and agents of God's will.

What you receive through them is not *their* energy, but purely that which is the Spirit's, through which they live within the Spirit's lucid world. Their task is to *transform* the Spirit's power, of which you could not otherwise become aware while living in the mortal creature's earthly darkness.

None of them assumes he is a "higher" being than you are; for everything they once might have *assumed* has been dissolved in the reality through which they *are*.

If you, however, feel that this reality is of a higher order than yourself, then be assured that also they experienced it to be above all else which, in their earthly lives, they might have felt desirable, or in their power to attain. They do not covet gratitude from those they help, and all their *helping* is effected by virtue purely of their *being*.

Nor can they bring you any other help than what you need if you resolve to reach your living God within you. If spiritual help is offered you even in other things you ought not to assume your *elder brothers* here on earth might be its source.

Indeed, within the Spirit's realm there also is found other help; and in their days on earth their own need of such help is often great.

Neither "super"-men nor fairy tale magicians, they are made subject in their days on earth to all the sufferings of mortal life the same way as are you; and in their having to endure, in all respects, this earthly life like other mortals, they recognize great wisdom.

How could they rescue souls that here abide in darkness to liberate them from this earthly night by the compassionate profusion of all the Spirit's energy that overflows their being if they were strangers to what mortal humans suffer?

By being witnesses of everything that mortals must endure they cause the Spirit's energy to be transformed in such a way that souls who need it on their path to God are able to receive and apprehend it according to their needs.

You truly may have trust in them, especially since nothing more is asked of you than not in any manner to reject their help.

Otherwise your *will*—expressed in such rejection—would of necessity prevent their help.

But if you are prepared and willing to be helped, then help will reach you on your path without request and pleading; for it does not depend upon the helper's whim.

Truly, one *must* find you—if you are willing to be found.

With certainty you then shall also find the truth which until now you had so often sought in vain.

You thus will comprehend what time and time again my words would to your soul convey: that only as *reality* can final truth be found.

⚬

CHAPTER FIVE

YES AND NO

YOU HARDLY CAN EXPECT TO FIND YOUR path to God as long as in your earthly life your "yes" and "no" are not determined by precise, inviolable limits.

Your "yes" and "no" must not receive direction simply by your wishes' ever-changing goals.

Even less so must your creature instincts' power govern your decision where you will say "yes," or "no."

On your decisiveness depends your fate's direction, and you alone will have to bear the consequences of each choice you make.

ONCE YOU HAVE resolved to free yourself from the dimension of *appearance*, so that through your works you may awaken and perceive *reality*, whatever still might tempt you to appear what you are *not*, must always be rejected by your "no."

Once you have decided to pursue the path to God, your "yes" no longer must provide support for anything that might prevent you from abiding at the highest levels of your soul.

Your "yes" and "no" can fortify your will, so that it may stand solid like a rock amidst the turmoil of external life.

Perhaps until this day you were not used to thinking that your "yes" and "no" were of such critical importance?

As prompted by your wishes, your "no" would readily become a "yes," your "yes" a "no."

But how, indeed, could that have been avoided, since you were searching aimlessly in all directions, but could not find the path your every effort truly wanted to discover?

Yet here that path is shown to you, and so your aimless search has ended.

Few things now shall prove of more importance than your "yes" or "no."

You must decide yourself in such a way that nothing henceforth shall be able to uproot your "yes," nor to corrupt your "no."

Before your "yes" and "no" have thus been firmly anchored in yourself, you carefully will have to weigh what is to be accepted by your "yes," and what excluded by your "no."

But then no earthly might should any longer have the power to reverse your "yes" or "no."

Even if you still should err, once having gained your self-determination your errors will mean little so long as they were purely caused by your intent to reach your highest goal.

Only lack of self-determination is of evil; only indecision leads to lasting harm.

SURELY, EVEN IN the days to come you never will be short of reasons that make you wish your self-defining "yes" and "no" were interchangeable; and sometimes you no doubt would rather let ambivalence become your refuge.

Therefore you should wisely search your motives before you choose your self-determination;

because each day confronts you with its question, demanding that you answer "yes" or "no"; and every day's new question will receive its answer by your changeless "yes" or by your equally unchanging "no."

And in the same way you determined your own being in view of that dimension where your self-determination shall abide forever, so must you likewise, true to your own self, each day anew decide your "yes" and "no" in all determinations of your earthly life.

You ought not to expect that you will reach your highest inner life as long as you are still uncertain whether your decision should be "yes" or "no."

You ought not to expect that you will reach your highest inner life the while your "yes" remains subservient to your mortal creature's instincts, where only "no" could set you free from bondage.

At a time of careful self-examination ask yourself, without evasion, what until now had found approval by your "yes," or was rejected by your "no."

Then, however, also ask yourself where until now you had avoided making a decision, allowing you a choice of saying sometimes "yes," and sometimes "no," according to your nature's murky cravings.

Do not be shocked if you are forced to see that, for its larger part, your house is built on quite unstable ground.

Instead, your task will now be to examine the ground on which its fundaments are set, so that you may secure it everywhere by solid footings and supports.

But here we also can dispense with images of figurative speech.

Your goal is to attain a firm determination of your will, which henceforth shall decide what is to be accepted by your "yes," and what your "no" should sever from your life.

It is not a question of your "embracing" or "renouncing" all the "world"; it is exclusively a matter of your own, quite narrowly constricted, earthly life, and how it should be lived.

You should resolve to live your life in such a way that everything that may uplift your inner self toward light and heightened purity is certain to receive your "yes," while all things bound to lower and demean you shall invariably face your "no."

Once you are yourself determined in this way, each decision you might have to make will then be "on its own" decided by the same determination.

The "yes" or "no" decisions in your daily life will simply be reflections of that which in your inner self is sanctioned by your "yes" or banished by your "no."

Make every effort, then, to strengthen and secure your "yes" and "no"!

No other task is here of more concern.

EVEN WHEN YOU have determined your own self, so that external influences are no longer able to determine *you*, that does not force you to become inflexible.

A decision that you make today may well deserve your "yes," while it tomorrow may demand your "no."

Today your "no" may raise and free you from the deep, where only "yes" will let you rise tomorrow.

Indeed, as you are growing, you will often have to change how you decide.

But once your self-determination is decided for all time, there always shall be found consistency in every change.

Within yourself, you shall not waver in such changes from the "yes" and "no" you made your own; and no matter how you may decide in any given case, all your decisions will be governed by your constant self-determination.

Judging from without, how you decide today may differ from tomorrow, given that external circumstances may have changed; but even then your "yes" and "no" must be decided by yourself alone—by virtue of the self-determination that you gave yourself, once and for all time, when you imposed forever settled limits upon your all-deciding "yes" and "no."

It will not do that you delude yourself to let your "yes" today become your "no" tomorrow, merely because your creature comfort or your wishes' bent would like to have you alter your decision.

Nor should any other person's "yes" and "no" be able to reverse your own when you have once attained the self-determination that your highest goal demands.

He that wants no more from life than to indulge his earthly creature's appetites will be directed by a different "yes" and "no" from someone who devotes his days on earth to the pursuit of the profoundest insights granted by his intellect.

And different again will be the "yes" and "no" that motivate the fool who serves an idol of his own creation.

You, however, who in yourself would find and take the path to God, will have to make a "yes" and "no" your guide that worthily reflects your lofty goal.

The "yes" and "no" that others made their own will help you nothing on your quest, even if you felt profound respect for them as persons; unless, that is, they had already found what you have just begun to seek, and thus could tell you how your "yes" and "no" must clearly be determined in yourself, that one day also you shall reach your goal, like them.

There will be few whose "yes" and "no" you might find helpful in this way.

More numerous by far you will find those whose aim is to determine—to mold—your will according to their own designs, while yet themselves devoid of any self-determination, be their purpose good or ill.

Such will prove your greatest peril, because you do not recognize their state of indetermination.

You should avoid them even more than all who mock your lofty goal, because their low determination knows and values only base pursuits.

Where you clearly recognize the "yes" of others as your own determined "no" you have no more to fear than where their "yes" and "no" is in complete accord with yours, to the extent that this is possible.

Beware of all, however, who constantly will tell you what they think you want to hear!

Beware of all who aim their speech at saying "no," but when they sense that you expected "yes," will quickly change their tune to end their words with "yes."!

Beware of all who can at any time change every "yes" to "no" and every "no" to "yes!"

No less beware, however, of any inclination to force your own determined "yes" and "no" on others!

The self-determination you attained is to be yours alone; others, to be sure, may in their own way come to be like you.

The only thing you can determine is yourself; you cannot rule the world outside.

When you attempt it nonetheless, and thus exceed your proper sphere, you will be grasping merely empty air, even though you would like to persuade yourself that you were able also to determine others.

To be sure, you can make others go astray and have them take your "yes" and "no" as theirs, while they are not determined yet within themselves; but if you thought that thus they had found self-determination, your vanity would have deluded you.

Very different from such delusion is the knowledge of the ways whereby your own determination continuously influences that of others, from within, whether this be your intent or not.

You cannot wholly isolate yourself from others in this life, even if you meant to flee into the desert, or built yourself a shelter in the deepest jungle.

Even if from this day on you never saw another soul, you nonetheless would always stay connected very closely with the human world.

By virtue of *invisible vibrations*, which at all times serve as faithful messengers of everything you may experience, feel, and think, you are continuously in connection, regardless of the distance, with all whose nature is akin to yours, and in the same way also you receive the messages which they transmit.

Although you may not be aware of these events, the constant workings of reality are not affected either by your knowing or your lack of knowledge.

All who seek their goal on kindred paths will thereby help each other.

So, too, shall you be helping others who seek their self-determination if you endeavor to determine your own self.

Your self-determined "yes" and "no" shall thus give help to others on their quest to find their own determination.

❧

CHAPTER SIX

THE DECISIVE BATTLE

T<small>HAT TO THIS DAY YOU HAVE NOT FOUND</small> God in yourself, to be united with the Living One in his eternal light, may serve you as sufficient proof that you are still in bondage to another's power, who neither is your God, nor your own self.

Unyielding are the chains that bind you, and only after having fought a long and bitter battle can you sever them to free yourself.

First, however, there is need to know who is your adversary in this battle.

H<small>E THAT HOLDS YOU</small> fast in unseen chains remains invisible himself, and willingly he lets you venerate him as a "God" and offer him your sacrifices. You can feel that he exists, but never will you comprehend his nature.

He certainly is not an idol of your own creation, nor does he draw his power merely from your faith.

And he is also not, as ancient dogma taught, God's "adversary" and his foe; since God to him does not exist; and all belief in things divine he merely scorns as human folly.

When he sees that human beings long for God he will present himself as that which they desire; for he knows but himself as "God." Yet when he recognizes that mortals seek instead to take a path that would enable them to break his chains, he turns into their most ferocious enemy and wants their earthly lives to be destroyed.

If his might were not confined by even higher powers, no human being would be able to experience God in mortal life.

AMONG THE FEW that have gained freedom from that unseen ruler's bondage there was one who in his day described him as the "prince of darkness." But those who heard him did not know of whom he spoke, nor do you know it even now.

Unless one chose to treat this saying merely as symbolic speech, one let imagination visualize as bogeyman, enough to frighten children, and found this concept adequate.

The entity, however, which the title "prince of darkness" signifies in the precise conception of that Master's saying, truly is a "prince of cosmic night." Notwithstanding that his reign has been substantially diminished by the very man who first defined him by that name.

We here are told about a being that objectively exists in the invisible dimension of the physically experienced cosmos; a being to whom all things on earth—to the extent they are of earthly substance—remain subjected in their earthly nature until that entity itself, together with this planet, shall finally disintegrate: become dissolved into unconscious cosmic energy.

With everything comprising your material, earthly nature, which includes not only your ability to think, but likewise all mechanical inventions that mortal humans ever have created, or shall develop in the future, your life is thoroughly within that being's power.

He is the "lord of earthly nature," and therefore also your own mortal nature's lord. You thus could truly worship him as "God"—if you were nothing more than a material creature of this earth.

Only the fact that you are more than merely an earth-born mortal creature allows you to escape his hold and raise yourself—in your eternal essence—above the one who in the end shall cease to be.

However, with your earthly body's nature you are subject to his power even then; but solely as a mortal who no longer is inevitably under his control, although at times you will be painfully aware of its effect.

To CHALLENGE the authority of this all-dominating cosmic ruler is a fateful undertaking.

More than merely human "courage" is required to contend with him in battle!

And yet you must initiate and make it through this contest, which will not end until the day when the material creature body in whose form you live shall separate itself from you and from your timeless essence.

Many have already perished on that field of battle who had made bold to wage this war with pompous pride but did not know with whom they fought.

Here, too, you are in need of higher help if you would see your victory secure as long as you still live on earth.

The site of battle here is not by any means exclusively within you.

Also from without you will be facing fierce assaults, and you continuously have to prove yourself—by virtue solely of your resolute *defense*; for the commencement of this battle on your part can never be *attack*, but only the rejection of the lord who rules the mortal creature, which henceforth is to serve you as an earthly tool, while earlier you had subjected even your eternal essence to that ruler's might.

Never shall the prince who rules the dark domain of matter willingly relinquish what is subject to his reign, but which you nonetheless must make obedient to your will if you desire, already in your life on earth, to find your God within you.

Nor will he ever "comprehend" the purpose of your quest, except as willful hubris; because to him all things pertaining to the Spirit, and that includes your God, are nothing more than mental fantasies, peculiar to the only ones among all earthborn creatures that are subject to his power, who nonetheless to him seem strange and alien.

He never shall himself engage you in this battle.

For that he deems you too contemptible a foe. Even in battle he remains the mortal creature's "prince" and thus will only have his vassals challenge you.

Quite unequal, then, will be this battle, in which a single combatant must constantly oppose a host of foes, many of whom alone would far exceed a mortal human's power unless he were continuously strengthened by the Spirit's higher might.

FAR-REACHING CONSEQUENCES will follow the day on which your inner being rises against the rule of that invisible prince of this world, and you resolve, from now on for all time, no longer to obey that ruler's will, who counts among his own devoted legions also those who had been *masters* of eternal Light, before their abject "fall" into the deep.

At first it well may seem to you as if all this were little more than simply acting in a harmless children's play, which you are staging for yourself, without the least effect in the invisible dimensions.

Soon enough, however, you will change your mind and clearly recognize with whom you henceforth are at war.

Yet no matter what you may have to contend with, be confident and steadfast in the knowledge that higher help is ever near you, even when you feel convinced that your defeat is certain.

You cannot ever be defeated the while your faith in victory is solely built upon the Spirit's might.

Those who succumbed in this conflict were always too convinced of their own strength, so that the Spirit's power could not take part and help them in their struggle.

Only if you let the Spirit's power join you in this battle will it grant you its support.

It is not those least capable, nor such as lack the needed courage, who are reluctant to accept assistance in this conflict.

It is not always self-conceit that makes a human being think he can decide the outcome of this battle on his own.

Even so, it is without exception an error of short-sighted judgment if anyone assumes that in this conflict he can triumph without the Spirit's help.

Believing this, he cannot be assisted, even if he sorely needs the Spirit's help, because through all his actions he rejects the very help that wants to end the conflict in his favor.

Those who here would see that victory is won on their behalf must never seek to gain it on their own.

With gratitude must they accept the triumph that the Spirit's power will award them.

They never must forget that their *resolve* to fight this battle is the only thing the Spirit's world demands of them, but that the Spirit's might alone is able to decide this conflict.

Those, however, who believe that they can triumph on their own do not have any concept of the prize that is to crown this battle; they do not recognize that nothing less is here at stake than seizing a component of the earth, and wresting it from earthly bondage, so that it may become united with the Spirit.

To be sure, even after victory is won by spiritual power, you will remain subservient to the "prince of this world" with your material body's nature as long as you still live on earth —but only that which one day shall decay must then still bear his rule.

Yet everything you made your own in life on earth beyond the substance that must needs disintegrate—however you prefer to call it— continues to belong to you even after your body's physical death; and it shall then be part of you, a self that is immortal, for all eternities to come.

Enter then this conflict with resolve and trust, knowing that you can prevail by virtue only of the Spirit's might supporting your— defense.

Victory is certain to be yours, if you but let the Spirit's power join you in this battle.

To be sure, you are expected to perform your part therein; your "part,", however, is at all times solely the *rejection* of the earthly demon's cosmic might, together with your will's reversal of direction: to offer him *resistance*—continuously, every instant of your further life on earth.

If you consistently perform your part, your victory is granted by the Spirit's power. You then will learn to unify all that which of your earthly nature is not subject to decay with your eternal self—forever.

Thus, unified within, you can no longer lose the path that leads to God, until one day you reach that path's exalted goal within you.

CHAPTER SEVEN

INDIVIDUAL PERFECTION

ONE COULD NOT FIND TWO HUMAN BEINGS on this earth who are alike in every way.

But even as the future figuration of a plant already lies embodied in its seed, so every human spirit bears within its essence the primordial image of its attainable perfection.

Infinitely many are the forms of life wherein God's self-experience comprehends itself.

Infinitely manifold are the reflections of the Godhead's life revealed in human spirits.

Infinitely many are the forms that manifest perfection.

Your individual perfection is the only one you can attain within yourself; and that of any other may give you merely an incentive to pursue your own in your own way.

The perfection reached by others is not yours, nor can it ever fill the void of what you fail to realize within yourself.

Let, then, eternal light become your guide that you may recognize the form that only in yourself demands to be perfected.

Put aside all vanity, all pride, and all ambition lest you lead yourself astray and strive for the perfection that another only can attain, while judging yours of little worth. Even the greatest among the perfected could not achieve any form but his own; and once perfected in your way, you shall be his equal in perfection.

Had he striven after greatness, knowing that among the perfect some were great, he truly never would have reached his own.

May your ambition let you scale the highest rung your gifts can reach in outer life, but keep it far from your pursuit of spiritual perfection!

IF IN YOURSELF you would discover the perfection that you alone are able to attain, you need to know that only when you are united with your God can you accomplish that perfection in yourself.

That is why I show you here the path to God, so that united with your God you one day shall attain perfection.

Not until you live your life united with your God will it in God become perfected.

It will at all times be your own distinctive life which in this way shall gain fulfillment.

You cannot ever live God's life; God, however, lives in you, and being unified with God you will be able to unfold your own life's highest form.

The following comparison may help your understanding.

Consider the lamp in which electric energy will cause a thread, no thicker than a hair, to glow and be a source of light.

You still are like the lamp not yet connected to the current's flow.

But when you shall one day be unified with God, you will be like a lamp whose innermost, which otherwise is barely visible, becomes a source of radiant light.

The lamp as such can never cause itself to glow.

Not until the current's power is connected with its inmost self can it display its radiance.

If the lamp could feel *itself*, however, it always would be conscious only of its inmost being—even though infused by light where once it had been dark—and only in that inmost self could it be likewise conscious of the power flowing through its essence.

Also you shall in that way experience purely your own inmost self when you one day shall be united with your living God.

Then shall your inmost essence shine in radiant clarity, enlivened by the Godhead's living light.

It does not mean that you have now become a "God," but that God's current flows through all your being.

In all eternity you can experience only your own self, and that which in yourself becomes your own experience.

THIS COMPARISON WILL also show you what I mean by saying that you can attain perfection only within God, and that no other soul's perfection can ever bring about your own.

The lamp through which the current does not flow may well be formed to manifest a light of wondrous nature, and yet it cannot shine. Its perfection will not be apparent until it is connected to the current's power.

And so can even you do everything required to attain perfection, but only when you shall be unified with God will you in truth achieve it.

And assuming many lamps were brought together in one place, only those connected to the current's force would ever shine.

The radiance of those burning lamps will never cause an unconnected lamp to shine.

And you as well can find perfection only by your striving to perfect yourself according to your own potential; and the perfection others have attained is of no help to you while you have not yourself gained union with your God.

Bear in mind, the task is finding your eternal life within yourself.

Only by perfecting that which needs to reach perfection in yourself will you be able to discern that timeless life.

You are to grow aware of it even as you are aware of your external life; and never shall you lose the consciousness of your eternal life if once you have attained it in yourself.

Decide, then, on your own whether the attainment of so high a goal does not seem worthy of your every effort!

At times you surely will have need to summon all your energies to keep that goal in sight.

Much, indeed, is being asked of you that the desires of your mortal creature will resist and which may be in conflict with your earthly wishes.

And yet, with all of your exertions you never would attain that goal but for the help that goal is granting you.

Ultimately, therefore, everything depends on your preparedness to accept such help.

The path's beginning, middle, and its goal are in yourself; and likewise in yourself alone shall highest help be offered you.

You then will feel your strength increasing day by day; and what at first you may have found too difficult a task, so that you all but lost your courage, shall no longer need much effort as you make progress on your path.

The closer you come to your goal, the more support you will be given, and the more distinctly will you feel that help.

Thus your energies will grow as you proceed, even as the path continues to get steeper, until at last you reach the sacred mountain's peak.

There shall all your toils and labors end.

Yet do not think that now there will be nothing more for you to find!

Infinite remains what you have found and new things you will find in it through all eternity.

In union with your God you shall perfect what in yourself alone was meant to find perfection; and thus you shall yourself become a trove of boundless wealth that will not be exhausted in infinity.

Then shall the Spirit's world, the realm of radiant substance, reveal its wonders to you more and more, and as you rise from joy to ever greater joy you will become aware that even in your days on earth you find yourself already in the very midst of your eternal life.

Within yourself you then have found what you had once been searching for in spheres beyond the clouds, but there could never find.

Perfected, then, you will release what must decay to earthly dissolution, for out of substance incorruptible you shall be born anew in God.

Thus you shall in truth have found your everlasting refuge.

Your path to God was but the journey to your own perfection.

❦

REMINDER

"Yet here I must point out again that if one would derive the fullest benefit from studying the books I wrote to show the way into the Spirit, one has to read them in the original; even if this should require learning German.

"Translations can at best provide assistance in helping readers gradually perceive, even through the spirit of a different language, what I convey with the resources of my mother tongue."

From "Answers to Everyone" (1933), *Gleanings*. Bern: Kobersche Verlags-buchhandlung, 1990

Other Works by Bô Yin Râ published in English translation:

Bô Yin Râ:
An Introduction to His Works

Contents: Preface. About My Books. Concerning My Name. In My Own Behalf. Essential Distinction. Résumé. Comments on the Cycle <Hortus Conclusus> and the Related Works. Brief Biography of Bô Yin Râ. The Works of Bô Yin Râ.

The Kober Press, 2004, 117 pages, paperback. ISBN 0-915034-10-7

This book presents a summary of the essential features that set the author's works on final things apart from the innumerable publications, old and new, that seek to answer questions which thinking minds have asked in every generation. Traditionally, such answers draw upon beliefs, accepted faith, and speculative thought, culminating in systems of religion and philosophy. Rarely have solutions rested on objective insights into the dynamic structure of reality, embracing both its physical and spiritual dimensions. But in addition to providing such direct descriptions of these aspects of reality, the author's books are helpful guides that let the readers gradually develop their inherent faculties so that they may experience this reality themselves. For readers having sensed the nature of this ultimate experience the concepts "spirit," "soul," "eternal life," and "God" are then no longer merely abstract notions based on hope and faith, but have become realities that form the human being's timeless essence, even as they underlie all aspects of creation.

In the first chapter of this *Introduction* the author discusses the origin and purpose of his books; how they should be used; for whom they are intended, and what their application may accomplish. Here he also stresses that his writings neither are opposed to, nor written to support, any particular religious creed, even though the followers of all persuasions may benefit from what they have to offer to all who seek to know.

The following chapter sheds light on the author's name and explains why his books are published under this spiritual proper name, which is not an arbitrary pseudonym, invented for the purpose of effective self-illumination, but expresses, in phonetic equivalents, the essence of his nature.

In the final chapter he corrects a number of misunderstandings of his books and person, typically prompted by hasty judgments, hearsay, or prejudice. Here he also touches on the common source of all authentic spiritual disclosures and stresses that objective insights into that dimension ought to be distinguished from the subjective mystical visions found in the different forms of religion.

The Book on the Royal Art

Contents: PART ONE: The Light from Himavat and the Words of the Masters. 1. The Luminary's Self-Disclosure to the Seeking Soul. 2. The Harvest. 3. The One whose Being is Infinity. 4. Know Thyself. 5. On the Masters of the Spirit's World. 6. Pitfalls of Vanity. PART TWO: From the Lands of the Luminaries. 1. The Threshold. 2. The King's Question. 3. The Pillar in the Mountains. 4. The Night of Easter. 5 Communion. PART THREE: The Will to Joy. 1. To All who Strive Toward Timeless Light. 2. The Teachings on Joy. Epilogue.

The Kober Press, 2006. 198 pages, paperback. ISBN 0-915034-13-1

This work is the first volume of *The Gated Garden*, a cycle of thirty-two books in which the author shows the way that lets his readers find objective spiritual truth within the light that darkness cannot conquer. In this opening volume the author discloses his own spiritual origin and sources and explains the reason leading to the publication of these books in our time. As the Western mediator of the oldest roots of ancient Eastern wisdom he also gives his readers the criteria to distinguish spurious echoes of that wisdom.

Of particular significance for Western readers is the chapter "The Night of Easter," which recalls the actual events preceding what would later be accepted as the Resurrection. In this context the book also touches on the Eastern wellspring in the teachings of the historical Master of Nazareth.

The concept "Royal Art" in the book's title refers to the Indian Raja Yoga, but here the term is used to denote a spiritual craft that far transcends the practices that are today suggested by that name.

As the portal to *The Gated Garden* this book is of particular importance in that is sets the tone and outlines the perspective from which all other volumes in the cycle should be viewed and understood.

The Book on the Living God

Contents: Word of Guidance. "The Tabernacle of God is with Men." The "Mahatmas" of Theosophy. Meta-Physical Experiences. The Inner Journey. The En-Sof. On Seeking God. On Leading an Active Life. On "Holy Men" and "Sinners." The Hidden Side of Nature. The Secret Temple. Karma. War and Peace. The Unity among Religions. The Will to Find Eternal Light. Mankind's Higher Faculties of Knowing. On Death. On the Spirit's Radiant Substance. The Path toward Perfection. On Everlasting Life. The Spirit's Light Dwells in the East. Faith, Talismans, and Images of God. The Inner Force in Words. A Call from Himavat. Giving Thanks. Epilogue.

The Kober Press, 1991. 333 pages, paperback. ISBN 0-915034-03-4

This work is the central volume of the author's *The Gated Garden*, a cycle of thirty-two books that let the reader gain a clear conception of the structure, laws, and nature of eternal life, and its reflections here on earth. The present work sheds light on the profound distinction between the various ideas and images of "God" that human faith has molded through the ages —as objects for external worship—and the eternal *spiritual reality*, which human souls are able to experience, even in this present life. How readers may attain this highest of all earthly goals; what they must do, and what avoid; and how their mortal life can be transformed into an integrated part of their eternal being, are topics fully treated in these pages.

What sets this author's works on spiritual life apart from other writings on the subject is their objective clarity, which rests upon direct perception of eternal life and its effects on human life on earth. Such perception is only possible, as he points out, if the observer's *spiritual* senses are as thoroughly developed to perceive realities of timeless life, as earthly senses need to be in order to experience *physical* existence. Given that authentic insights gathered in this way have always been extremely rare, they rank among the most important writings of their time, conveying knowledge of enduring worth that otherwise would not become accessible.

The Book on Life Beyond

Contents: Introduction. The Art of Dying. The Temple of Eternity and the World of Spirit. The Only Absolute Reality. What Should One Do?

The Kober Press, 2002. 161 pages, paperback. ISBN 0-915034-11-5.

This book explains why life "beyond" is not so much a different and wholly other life, but rather the continuation of the self-same life we live on earth. The difference between the two dimensions lies chiefly in the organs of perception through which the same reality of life is individually experienced. On earth we know that life through our mortal senses, in life beyond it is perceived through spiritual faculties, which typically awaken after death. At that transition, the human consciousness, which usually is unprepared for the event, is at a loss and finds itself confused by the beliefs and concepts of its former mortal life. As a result, the new arrival faces certain dangers; for, owing to these mental prejudices, the person is unable to distinguish between perceptions of objective truth and the alluring phantom "heavens" generated by misguided faith on earth.

To help perceptive readers form correct and realistic expectations, that they may one day reach the other shore with confidence and without fear, this book provides trustworthy guidance into spiritual life, its all-pervading structure, laws, and inner nature. Given the unbreakable connection between our actions here on earth and their effects on life beyond, the book advises how this present life may best prepare the reader for the life that is to come.

The Book on Human Nature

Contents: Introduction. The Mystery Enshrouding Male and Female. The Path of the Female. The Path of the Male. Marriage. Children. The Human Being of the Age to Come. Epilogue. A Final Word.

The Kober Press, 2000, 168 pages, paperback, ISBN 0-915034-07-7

Together with *The Book on the Living God* and *The Book on Life Beyond*, *The Book on Human Nature* forms a trilogy containing guidelines toward a new and more objective understanding of both physical and spiritual realities, and of the human being's origin and place within these two dimensions of creation.

The Book on Human Nature at the outset shows the need to draw a clear distinction between the timeless spiritual component present in each mortal human, and the material creature body in which the spiritual essence is embodied during mortal life. The former, indestructible and timeless, owing to its being born of spiritual substance, represents the truly human element in what is known as mortal man. The latter, physical, contingent, and subject to decay and death, is no more than the temporary instrument the spiritual being uses to express itself in physical existence. Given that the spiritual and animal components within human nature manifest inherently discordant aspects of reality, they typically contend for domination of the total individual. Experience shows that in this conflict the animal component with its ruthless drives and instincts clearly proves the stronger.

To help the reader gain a realistic understanding of the human being's spiritual and physical beginnings, by way of concepts more in keeping with humanity's advances in every discipline of natural science, the book explains, to the extent that metaphysical events can be conveyed through language, the timeless origin and source of every human's spiritual descent. It likewise shows that the material organism, now considered mankind's primal ancestor, existed long before it was to serve the spiritual individuation as its earthly tool. In this context the author points out that the traditional creation story, such as it has survived, is not simply an archaic myth, invented at a time that lacked the benefits of modern knowledge, but instead preserves, in lucid images and symbols, a truthful view of actual events. Events, however, that did not happen merely once, at the beginning of creation, but are a process that continues even now, and will recur until this planet can no longer nurture human life.

Even so, the principal intention of the present work, as well as of the author's other expositions of reality, is not so much to offer readers a new, reliable cosmology, but rather to encourage them to rediscover and awaken the spiritual nature in themselves, and thus to live their present and their future life as fully conscious, truly human beings.

The Book on Happiness

Contents: Prelude. Creating Happiness as Moral Duty. "I" and "You". Love. Wealth and Poverty. Money. Optimism. Conclusion.

The Kober Press, 1994. 127 pages, paperback. ISBN 0-915034-04-2.

Sages and philosophers in every age and culture have speculated on the nature, roots, and attributes of happiness, and many theories have sought to analyze this enigmatic subject. In modern times, psychology has joined the search for concrete answers with its own investigations, which frequently arrive at findings that support established views. Still, the real essence of true happiness remains an unsolved riddle.

In contrast to traditional approaches, associating happiness with physical events, the present book points to the spiritual source from which all human happiness derives, both in life on earth and in the life to come. Without awareness of this nonmaterial fundament, one's understanding of true happiness is bound to be deficient.

The author shows that real happiness is neither owing to blind chance, nor a capricious gift of luck, but rather the creation of determined human will. It is an inner state that must be fostered day by day; for real happiness, as it is here defined, is "the contentment that creative human will enjoys in its creation." How that state may be created and sustained, in every aspect of this life, the reader can discover in this book.

The Book on Love

Contents: Introduction. The Greatest of Compassion's Mediators. On Love's Primordial Fire. Light of Liberation. On Love's Creative Power.

The Kober Press,. 2005. 148 pages, paperback. ISBN 978-0-915034-12-3

Love, properly understood, is not merely, as the author explains, a human sentiment of varying degrees of intensity, inspired by particular objects and, like all feelings, subject to continuous change. Love is, instead, the highest of creation's elemental powers, giving life to and sustaining all dimensions of reality. The human sentiment called "love" is but a faint reflection of that cosmic force and ought to be distinguished clearly from its distant source.

Earthly love in all its forms is typically aroused by the desire of possession for an object. Celestial love, by contrast, is a spiritual energy that manifests itself beyond and free of all desire, independent of external objects. Human beings can partake of the celestial form of love, which then transforms their temporal existence by virtue of their timeless life, and thus will make them more than simply "sounding brass and tinkling cymbals."

In its initial chapter the book sheds light on the historical facts surrounding the life and teachings of the unprecedented figure of Jesus of Nazareth, who, more perfectly than anyone before or since, embodied love's celestial force in word and deed. Empowered by that highest form of love he found the strength to change this planet's spiritual aura in his final hour and freed all human beings of good will from ancient bondage.

The Book on Solace

Contents: On Grief and Finding Solace. Lessons One Can Learn from Grief. On Follies to Avoid. On the Comforting Virtue of Work. On Solace in Bereavement.

The Kober Press, 1996. 126 pages, paperback. ISBN 0-915034-05-0.

In this book the author shows how sorrow, pain, and grief, although inevitable burdens of this present life, can and ought to be confronted and confined within the narrow borders of necessity. Considered from the spiritual perspective, all suffering experienced on this earth is the inexorable consequence of mankind's having willfully abandoned its given state of harmony within the Spirit, a deed that also ruined the perfection of material nature. Although the sum of grief thus brought upon this planet is immense, human beings needlessly expand and heighten its ferocity by foolishly regarding grief as something noble and refined, if not, indeed, a token of God's "grace."

Understanding pain objectively, as a defect confined to physical existence, which, even in exceptional cases, is but an interlude in every mortal's timeless life, allows the reader to perceive its burdens in a clearer light, and thus more patiently to bear it with resolve.

While suffering, through human fault, remains the tragic fate of physical creation, the highest source of solace, which helps the human soul endure its pain and sorrow, continually sends its comfort from the Spirit's world to all who seek it in themselves. How readers may discover and draw solace from that inner source the present book will show them.

The Book of Dialogues

Contents: Testimony. Knowledge and Reality in Action. Light and Darkness. The Spirit's Might. The Jewel of the Heart. Transformation. The Dialogue on the Innermost East. The Dialogue on the Passing of a Master. The Flower Garden. The Deviant Pupils. Night of Trial. Individuality and Person. The Realm of the Soul. On Finding Oneself. On the Elder Brothers of Mankind. Mystery of Magic.

The Kober Press, 2007. 175 pages, paperback. ISBN 978-0-915034-14-X

This book contains a series of conversations between the author as a pupil and his spiritual mentors, before he was himself accepted as a Master in their circle. It touches on a number of essential topics that help the reader recognize authentic knowledge of objective spiritual truth and the nature of those who, since the dawn of time, have conveyed that truth to humankind as spiritually sanctioned Mediators.

The book is of especial interest for its biographical disclosures, as these not merely shed unprecedented light on the development and schooling of authentic spiritual Mediators, but also on the singular position assigned to the author of the present and the other volumes of The Gated Garden.

As the Western representative and voice of the perennial Eastern source from which all timeless insights into spiritual light and knowledge flow, the author shows the way to those who have been guiding human spirits to eternal light since ages immemorial, long before the rise of temporal religious creeds.

While insights from that highest source have reached humanity in ancient days, time and misinterpretations have shrouded their authentic form, nor have they ever been presented to the public at large as an integrated whole in such detail before.

The Wisdom of St. John

Contents: Introduction. The Master's Image. The Luminary's Mortal Life. The Aftermath. The Missive. The Authentic Doctrine. The Paraclete. Conclusion.

The Kober Press, 1975. 92 pages, clothbound. ISBN 0-915034-01-8.

This exposition of the Fourth Gospel is not a scholarly analysis discussing the perplexing riddles of this ancient text. It is, instead, a nondogmatic reconstruction of the actual events recorded in that work, whose author wanted to present the truth about the Master's life and teachings; for the image propagated by the missionaries of the new religion often was in conflict with the facts. The present book restores the context of essential portions of the unknown author's secret missive, which the first redactors had corrupted, so that its contents would support the other gospels.

Written by a follower of John, the "beloved disciple," its purpose was to disavow the "miracles" the other records had ascribed to the admired teacher. His record also is unique in that it has preserved the substance of some letters by the Master's hand, addressed to that favorite pupil. Those writings are reflected in the great discourses which set this gospel text apart and lend it its distinctive tone.

Given the historic impact of the man presented in this work, an accurate conception of his life and message will not only benefit believers of the faith established in his name, but also may explain to others what his death in fact accomplished for mankind.

The Meaning of this Life

Contents: A Call to the Lost. The Iniquity of the Fathers. The Highest Goal. The "Evil" Individual. Summons from the World of Light. The Benefits of Silence. Truth and Verities. Conclusion.

The Kober Press, 1998, 126 pages, paperback. ISBN 0-915034-06-9.

This book addresses the most common questions people tend to ask at times when circumstances in their daily lives awaken their awareness of the many unsolved riddles that surround the human being here on earth. To be sure, philosophy and teachings of religion have offered answers to such questions through the ages, but as these often draw on speculation, or require blind belief, they can no longer truly satisfy the searching mind of our time.

It is against this background that the present book will guide its readers to a firmer ground of understanding, resting on objective insights and experience. From this solid vantage, readers may survey their own existence and its purpose with assurance.

As this book explains, the key to comprehending the meaning of this present life is, first, the insight that this life is but the consequence of causes in the Spirit's world and, thus, has of itself no meaning other than that fact. And, secondly, the recognition that material life is ultimately meaningless if human beings fail to give it meaning: by virtue of pursuing goals whose blessings shall endure. The nature of the highest goal that mortals can pursue provides the substance also of the present book.

Spirit and Form

Contents: The Question. Outer World and Inner Life. At Home and at Work. Forming One's Joy. Forming One's Grief. The Art of Living Mortal Life.

The Kober Press, 2000. 108 pages, paperback. ISBN 0-915034-07-7

The underlying lesson of this book is that all life in the domain of spiritual reality, from the highest to the lowest spheres, reveals itself as lucid order, form, and structure. Spirit, the all-sustaining radiant *substance* of creation, is in itself the final source and pattern of all perfect form throughout its infinite dimensions. Nothing, therefore, can exist within, or find admittance to, the Spirit's inner worlds that is devoid of the perfection, harmony, and structure necessarily prevailing in these spheres.

Given that this present life is meant to serve the human being as an effective preparation for regaining the experience of spiritual reality, this life must needs be lived in ways that are consistent with the principles that govern spiritual reality; in other words, ought to be lived according to the structure, laws, and inner forms of that reality. To show the reader how this present life receives enduring form, which then is able to survive this mortal state, the book sheds light on crucial aspects of this physical existence and advises how these may be formed to serve one's spiritual pursuits.

Worlds of Spirit
A Sequence of Cosmic Perspectives

Contents: Preface. The Ascent. The Return. Reviews of Creation. Epilogue.

Illustrations: *Emanation. In Principio erat Verbum. Lux in Tenebris. Te Deum Laudamus. Space and Time. Primal Generation. Seeds of Future Worlds. Emerging Worlds. Birth of the External Cosmos. Labyrinth. Desire for External Form. Astral Luminescence. Sodom. Inferno. De Profundis. Revelation. Illumination. Fulfillment. Victory. Himavat.*

The Kober Press, 2002. 96 pages, 20 full-color illustrations, hardcover. ISBN 0-915034-09-3.

If all the books of Bô Yin Râ, objectively considered, are unparalleled in the extensive literature on subjects touching final things—in that their author did not publish speculations based on faith or thought, but gave the reader fact-based insights into spiritual reality—the volume *Worlds of Spirit* occupies a special place even among these thirty-two unprecedented works; for in this book he integrated twenty reproductions of his paintings, representing *spiritual perspectives*, to illustrate selected aspects of his text.

While the works of the *Hortus Conclusus* cycle constitute the first authentic, comprehensive exposition of metaphysical realities, the paintings in this volume represent, in turn, the first objective visual renditions of spiritual dimensions in their dynamic figurations, colors, and inherent structure. Together with the written word—the book describes events experienced and perceived by an awakened human spirit—the images are meant to offer readers lucid concepts of nonphysical existence, and thereby to assist them in developing their own perceptive faculties.

❧

THE
KOBER
PRESS

www.ingramcontent.com/pod-product-compliance
Lightning Source LLC
Chambersburg PA
CBHW060400090426
42734CB00011B/2206